D0560850

Presented To:

_____

Presented By:

_____

Date:

_____

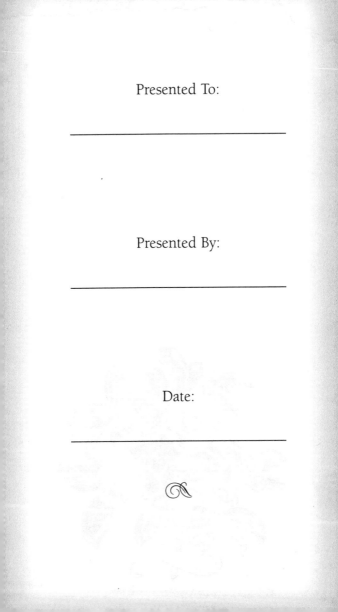

God's Little Book of
Promises
for Mothers

Honor Books
Tulsa, Oklahoma

God's Little Book of Promises for Mothers
ISBN 1-56292-497-4
Copyright © 1998 by Honor Books
P.O. Box 55388
Tulsa, Oklahoma 74155

References

Introduction

God's Word is filled with the promises He has made to His children. It is His desire that we understand His promises and His faithfulness to us. *God's Little Book of Promises for Mothers* is a book to help women do just that.

Arranged topically, this little book lists the truths given in God's Word about issues we face in our lives. Whether struggling financially, seeking to understand the role of wife and mother, or desiring to know more deeply the character of God, women of all ages and backgrounds can turn to a truth and a promise that is biblical.

God is faithful to His Word and eager to bring it to fullness in our lives. This book is designed to start us on the way and to keep us on the path.

Table of Contents

for Mothers

The Truth about Anger

He who is slow to anger has great
understanding, but he who is
quick-tempered exalts folly.
Proverbs 14:29 NASB

He that is slow to anger is better
than the mighty; and he that ruleth
his spirit than he that taketh a city.
Proverbs 16:32 KJV

Wherefore, my beloved brethren,
let every man be swift to hear,
slow to speak, slow to wrath:
for the wrath of man worketh
not the righteousness of God.
James 1:19-20 KJV

For we know him that hath said,
Vengeance belongeth unto me,
I will recompense, saith the Lord.
Hebrews 10:30 KJV

for Mothers

What To Do When You Are Angry

Be ye angry, and sin not: let not
the sun go down upon your wrath.
Ephesians 4:26 KJV

A soft answer turneth away wrath:
but grievous words stir up anger.
Proverbs 15:1 KJV

For if you forgive men
their trespasses, your heavenly
Father will also forgive you.
Matthew 6:14 NKJV

If is is possible, as
much as depends on you,
live peaceably with all men.
Romans 12:18 NKJV

How To Overcome Improper Anger

But now ye also put off all these;
anger, wrath, malice, blasphemy,
filthy communication out
of your mouth.
Colossians 3:8 KJV

Finally, brethren, whatsoever
things are true, whatsoever things
are honest, whatsoever things are
just, whatsoever things are pure,
whatsoever things are lovely,
whatsoever things are of good
report; if there be any virtue,
and if there be any praise,
think on these things.
Philippians 4:8 KJV

Accept one another, then,
just as Christ accepted you,
in order to bring praise to God.
Romans 15:7

God's Little Book of Promises
for Mothers

The Truth about Assurance

I, even I, am he who blots out your
transgressions, for my own sake,
and remembers your sins no more.
Isaiah 43:25

As far as the east is from the west,
so far has He removed our
transgressions from us.
Psalm 103:12 NKJV

All that the Father giveth me shall
come to me; and him that cometh
to me I will in no wise cast out.
John 6:37 KJV

Truly, truly, I say to you, he who
hears My word, and believes Him
who sent Me, has eternal life, and
does not come into judgment, but
has passed out of death into life.
John 5:24 NASB

for Mothers

Unshakable Assurance

For by grace you have been
saved through faith; and this
is not of your own doing,
it is the gift of God.
Ephesians 2:8 RSV

And I am sure that God who
began the good work within you
will keep right on helping you
grow in his grace until his task
within you is finally finished.
Philippians 1:6 TLB

My sheep hear my voice,
and I know them, and they follow
me: and I give unto them eternal
life; and they shall never perish,
neither shall any man pluck
them out of my hand.
John 10:27-28 KJV

How To Have Assurance

If you confess with your mouth,
"Jesus is Lord," and believe in your
heart that God raised him from
the dead, you will be saved.
Romans 10:9

In Him you also trusted, after you
heard the word of truth, the gospel
of your salvation; in whom also,
having believed, you were sealed
with the Holy Spirit of promise.
Ephesians 1:13 NJKV

Now He who establishes us with
you in Christ and anointed us
is God, who also sealed us
and gave us the Spirit in
our hearts as a pledge.
2 Corinthians 1:21-22 NASB

for Mothers

The Truth about Burdens

Do not be anxious about anything,
but in everything, by prayer and
petition, with thanksgiving,
present your requests to God.
And the peace of God, which
transcends all understanding,
will guard your hearts and
your minds in Christ Jesus.
Philippians 4:6-7

The Lord preserveth the simple:
I was brought low, and he helped
me. Return unto thy rest,
O my soul; for the Lord hath
dealt bountifully with thee.
For thou hast delivered my soul
from death, mine eyes from tears,
and my feet from falling.
Psalm 116:6-8 KJV

for Mothers

Comfort for Your Burdens

You therefore must endure
hardship as a good soldier
of Jesus Christ.
2 Timothy 2:3 NKJV

My brethren, count it all joy
when you fall into various trials.
James 1:2 NKJV

For I, the Lord your God, hold
your right hand; it is I who say to
you, "Fear not, I will help you."
Isaiah 41:13 RSV

These things I have spoken unto
you, that in me ye might have
peace. In the world ye shall have
tribulation: but be of good cheer;
I have overcome the world.
John 16:33 KJV

for Mothers

When You Carry Burdens

Cast thy burden upon the Lord,
and he shall sustain thee.
Psalm 55:22 KJV

Come to me, all you who are
weary and burdened, and I will
give you rest. Take my yoke upon
you and learn from me, for I am
gentle and humble in heart, and
you will find rest for your souls.
For my yoke is easy and
my burden is light.
Matthew 11:28-30

Therefore humble yourselves
under the mighty hand of God,
that He may exalt you in due time,
casting all your care upon Him,
for He cares for you.
1 Peter 5:6-7 NKJV

The Truth about Children

The promise is for you and
your children and for all
who are far off—for all whom
the Lord our God will call.
Acts 2:39

Let the children come to me,
for the Kingdom of God
belongs to such as they.
Don't send them away!
Mark 10:14 TLB

Children are a gift from God;
they are his reward. Children
born to a young man are like
sharp arrows to defend him.
Happy is the man who has
his quiver full of them.
Psalm 127:3-4 TLB

Parents and Children

Her children arise and
call her blessed.
Proverbs 31:28

A woman giving birth to
a child has pain because her
time has come; but when her baby
is born she forgets the anguish
because of her joy that a child
is born into the world.
John 16:21

For this child I prayed, and
the Lord has granted me my
petition which I asked of Him.
Therefore I also have lent him to
the Lord; as long as he lives he
shall be lent to the Lord.
1 Samuel 1:27-28 NKJV

for Mothers

Spiritual Training

And all thy children shall be
taught of the Lord; and great shall
be the peace of thy children.
Isaiah 54:13 KJV

Only take heed to yourself, and
dilgently keep yourself, lest you
forget the things your eyes have
seen, and lest they depart from
your heart all the days of your life.
And teach them to your children
and your grandchildren.
Deuteronomy 4:9 NKJV

Train a child in the way
he should go, and when he is old
he will not turn from it.
Proverbs 22:6

The Truth about Comfort

Blessed be the God and Father of
our Lord Jesus Christ, the Father
of mercies and God of all comfort,
who comforts us in all our
affliction so that we will be
able to comfort those who are in
any affliction with the comfort
with which we ourselves are
comforted by God.
2 Corinthians 1:3-4 NASB

But the Comforter, which is the
Holy Ghost, whom the Father will
send in my name, he shall teach
you all things, and bring all things
to your remembrance, whatsoever
I have said unto you.
John 14:26 KJV

The Lord is good, a refuge in
times of trouble. He cares for
those who trust in him.
Nahum 1:7

for Mothers

In Need of Comfort

Come to me, all who labor
and are heavy laden,
and I will give you rest.
Matthew 11:28 RSV

The Lord is a stronghold
for the oppressed, a stronghold
in times of trouble.
Psalm 9:9 RSV

Though I am surrounded
by troubles, you will bring me
safely through them.
Psalm 138:7 TLB

Don't be impatient. Wait for
the Lord, and he will come
and save you! Be brave,
stouthearted and courageous.
Yes, wait and he will help you.
Psalm 27:14 TLB

Comfort Is with You

For as the sufferings of Christ
abound in us, so our consolation
also abounds through Christ.
2 Corinthians 1:5 NKJV

Cast your cares on the Lord and
he will sustain you; he will
never let the righteous fall.
Psalm 55:22

For the Angel of the Lord guards
and rescues all who reverence him.
Psalm 34:7 TLB

Through the Lord's mercies
we are not consumed, because
His compassions fail not. They
are new every morning; great is
Your faithfulness. "The Lord is
my portion," says my soul,
"therefore I hope in Him!"
Lamentations 3:22-24 NKJV

for Mothers

The Truth about Commitment

As you therefore have received
Christ Jesus the Lord, so walk
in Him, rooted and built up in
Him and established in the faith,
as you have been taught,
abounding in it with thanksgiving.
Colossians 2:6-7 NKJV

For God hath not appointed us
to wrath, but to obtain salvation
by our Lord Jesus Christ.
1 Thessalonians 5:9 KJV

But we are bound to give thanks
alway to God for you, brethren
beloved of the Lord, because
God hath from the beginning
chosen you to salvation through
sanctification of the Spirit
and belief of the truth.
2 Thessalonians 2:13 KJV

Making the Commitment

Commit your way to the Lord,
trust also in Him, and He
shall bring it to pass. He shall
bring forth your righteousness
as the light, and your justice
as the noonday.
Psalm 37:5-6 NKJV

Therefore let those who
suffer according to the will
of God commit their souls
to Him in doing good,
as to a faithful Creator.
1 Peter 4:19 NKJV

Let your heart therefore be loyal
to the Lord our God, to walk
in His statutes and keep His
commandments, as at this day.
1 Kings 8:61 NKJV

Promises Come with Commitment

Ye are washed, but ye are
sanctified, but ye are justified in
the name of the Lord Jesus, and by
the Spirit of our God.
1 Corinthians 6:11 KJV

Commit your work to the Lord,
then it will succeed.
Proverbs 16:3 TLB

Commit everything you do to the
Lord. Trust him to help you do it
and he will. Your innocence will
be clear to everyone. He will
vindicate you with the blazing
light of justice shining down
as from the noonday sun.
Psalm 37:5-6 TLB

The Truth about Confidence

So we are always confident,
knowing that while we are at
home in the body we are absent
from the Lord. For we walk
by faith, not by sight.
2 Corinthians 5:6-7 NKJV

Let us then approach the throne of
grace with confidence, so that we
may receive mercy and find grace
to help us in our time of need.
Hebrews 4:16

We have confidence to enter the
holy place by the blood of Jesus.
Hebrews 10:19 NASB

For the Lord will be your
confidence, and will keep
your foot from being caught.
Proverbs 3:26 NKJV

for Mothers

The Place To Put Confidence

I would have lost heart, unless I
had believed that I would see the
goodness of the Lord in the land of
the living. Wait on the Lord; be of
good courage, and He shall
strengthen your heart; wait, I say,
on the Lord!
Psalm 27:13-14 NKJV

For it is we who are the
circumcision, we who worship by
the Spirit of God, who glory in
Christ Jesus, and who put no
confidence in the flesh.
Philippians 3:3

Beloved, if our heart
does not condemn us,
we have confidence before God.
1 John 3:21 NASB

Finding Confidence

And I am sure that God who
began the good work within you
will keep right on helping
you grow in his grace until
his task within you is finally
finished on that day
when Jesus Christ returns.
Philippians 1:6 TLB

Be strong and courageous, do not
be afraid or tremble at them,
for the Lord your God is the one
who goes with you. He will
not fail you or forsake you.
Deuteronomy 31:6 NASB

Last of all I want to remind you
that your strength must come
from the Lord's mighty
power within you.
Ephesians 6:10 TLB

The Truth about Conflict

I appeal to you, brethren, by the
name of our Lord Jesus Christ, that
all of you agree and that there be
no dissensions among you, but
that you be united in the same
mind and the same judgment.
1 Corinthians 1:10 RSV

And a servant of the Lord must not
quarrel but be gentle to all.
2 Timothy 2:24 NKJV

A wrathful man stirs up strife,
but he who is slow to anger
allays contention.
Proverbs 15:18 NKJV

for Mothers

Fighting Conflict

How good and pleasant it is when
brothers live together in unity!
Psalm 133:1

May the God of steadfastness and
encouragement grant you to live in
such harmony with one another,
in accord with Christ Jesus, that
together you may with one voice
glorify the God and Father of
our Lord Jesus Christ.
Romans 15:5-6 RSV

Try always to be led along together
by the Holy Spirit, and so be at
peace with one another.
Ephesians 4:3 TLB

And above all these things
put on charity, which is
the bond of perfectness.
Colossians 3:14 KJV

for Mothers

When You Face Conflict

Dare any of you,
having a matter against another,
go to law before the unrighteous,
and not before the saints?
1 Corinthians 6:1 NKJV

See that no one repays another
with evil for evil, but always seek
after that which is good for one
another and for all people.
1 Thessalonians 5:15 NASB

Don't grumble about each other,
brothers. Are you yourselves
above criticism? For see!
The great Judge is coming.
James 5:9 TLB

The Truth about Courage

Be of good courage, and
he shall strengthen your heart,
all ye that hope in the Lord.
Psalm 31:24 KJV

Be strong and courageous,
do not fear or be dismayed . . .
for the one with us is greater
than the one with him.
2 Chronicles 32:7 NASB

Yes, be bold and strong!
Banish fear and doubt!
For remember, the Lord your
God is with you wherever you go.
Joshua 1:9 TLB

Peace I leave with you;
My peace I give to you; not as
the world gives do I give to you.
John 14:27 NASB

for Mothers

Take Courage

Wait for the Lord; be strong,
and let your heart take courage;
yes, wait for the Lord.
Psalm 27:14 NASB

And so we should not be like
cringing, fearful slaves, but we
should behave like God's very
own children, adopted into the
bosom of his family, and calling
to him, "Father, Father."
Romans 8:15 TLB

The Lord is my light and my
salvation . . . whom shall I fear?
When evil men come to destroy
me, they will stumble and fall!
Yes, though a mighty army
marches against me, my heart
shall know no fear! I am
confident that God will save me.
Psalm 27:1-3 TLB

Where To Find Courage

He gives power to the tired and
worn out, and strength to the weak.
Isaiah 40:29 TLB

For I am the Lord, your God,
who takes hold of your
right hand and says to you,
Do not fear; I will help you.
Isaiah 41:13

That is why we can say
without any doubt or fear,
"The Lord is my Helper and
I am not afraid of anything
that mere man can do to me."
Hebrews 13:6 TLB

Overwhelming victory is ours
through Christ who loved us
enough to die for us.
Romans 8:37 TLB

The Truth about Death

When calamity comes, the wicked
are brought down, but even in
death the righteous have a refuge.
Proverbs 14:32

Truly, truly, I say to you,
if any one keeps my word
he will never see death.
John 8:51 RSV

I will ransom them from
the power of the grave; I will
redeem them from death.
Hosea 13:14 KJV

Whoever believes in Him should
not perish but have eternal life.
John 3:15 NKJV

Christ's Death

And since by his blood he
did all this for us as sinners, how
much more will he do for us now
that he has declared us not guilty?
Now he will save us from
all of God's wrath to come.
Romans 5:9 TLB

Since we, God's children,
are human beings—made of flesh
and blood—he became flesh and
blood too by being born in human
form; for only as a human being
could he die and in dying break
the power of the devil who had
the power of death.
Hebrews 2:14 TLB

He will swallow up death forever,
and the Lord God will wipe
away tears from all faces.
Isaiah 25:8 NKJV

Believers and Death

But God will ransom my soul
from the power of Sheol,
for he will receive me.
Psalm 49:15 RSV

But the good man—what
a different story! For the good
man—the blameless, the upright,
the man of peace—he has a
wonderful future ahead of him.
For him there is a happy ending.
Psalm 37:37 TLB

For to me, to live is Christ
and to die is gain.
Philippians 1:21

The Truth about Deliverance

Because he cleaves to me in love,
I will deliver him; I will protect
him, because he knows my name.
When he calls to me, I will answer
him; I will be with him in trouble,
I will rescue him and honor him.
Psalm 91:14-15 RSV

For he has rescued us out of
the darkness and gloom of Satan's
kingdom and brought us into
the Kingdom of his dear Son.
Colossians 1:13 TLB

The Lord knoweth how to deliver
the godly out of temptations, and
to reserve the unjust unto the day
of judgment to be punished.
2 Peter 2:9 KJV

God's Little Book of Promises

for Mothers

Receiving Deliverance

When the righteous cry for help,
the Lord hears, and delivers
them out of all their troubles.
Psalm 34:17 RSV

God blesses those who are kind
to the poor. He helps them
out of their troubles.
Psalm 41:1 TLB

He who trusts in his own heart
is a fool, but whoever walks
wisely will be delivered.
Proverbs 28:26 NKJV

Call to me and I will answer you,
and will tell you great and hidden
things which you have not known.
Jeremiah 33:3 RSV

for Mothers

The Deliverer

The Lord is my rock and my
fortress and my deliverer; my God,
my strength, in whom I will trust.
Psalm 18:2 NKJV

I call to the Lord, who is
worthy of praise, and I am
saved from my enemies.
Psalm 18:3

But I am poor and needy;
yet the Lord thinks upon me.
You are my help and my deliverer;
do not delay, O my God.
Psalm 40:17 NKJV

The Lord preserves the simple;
when I was brought low,
he saved me.
Psalm 116:6 RSV

The Truth about Discipline

But I keep under my body,
and bring it into subjection:
lest that by any means,
when I have preached to others,
I myself should be a castaway.
1 Corinthians 9:27 KJV

I have been crucified with Christ;
it is no longer I who live, but
Christ lives in me; and the life
which I now live in the flesh I live
by faith in the Son of God, who
loved me and gave Himself for me.
Galatians 2:20 NKJV

He that hath no rule over his
own spirit is like a city that is
broken down, and without walls.
Proverbs 25:28 KJV

Being Disciplined

Do not offer the parts of your
body to sin, as instruments of
wickedness, but rather offer
yourselves to God, as those
who have been brought
from death to life; and offer the
parts of your body to him as
instruments of righteousness.
Romans 6:13

Now your attitudes and thoughts
must all be constantly changing
for the better. Yes, you must be
a new and different person,
holy and good. Clothe yourself
with this new nature.
Ephesians 4:23-24 TLB

Put on the Lord Jesus Christ, and
make no provision for the flesh,
to fulfill its lusts.
Romans 13:14 NKJV

Discipline from God

Blessed is the man whom
God corrects; so do not despise
the discipline of the Almighty.
Job 5:17

Blessed is the man whom
You chasten, O LORD, and whom
You teach out of Your law.
Psalm 94:12 NASB

"I am with you and will save you,"
declares the Lord . . .
I will discipline you but
only with justice.
Jeremiah 30:11

As many as I love,
I rebuke and chasten.
Therefore be zealous and repent.
Revelation 3:19 NKJV

❧

The Truth about Discontentment

Out of heaven He let you hear His
voice, that He might instruct you.
Deuteronomy 4:36 NKJV

Now godliness with
contentment is great gain.
1 Timothy 6:6 NKJV

Let not thine heart envy sinners:
but be thou in the fear of the
Lord all the day long. For surely
there is an end; and thine
expectation shall not be cut off.
Proverbs 23:17-18 KJV

Seek the Lord and his strength,
seek his face continually.
Remember his marvellous works
that he hath done, his wonders,
and the judgments of his mouth.
1 Chronicles 16:11-12 KJV

for Mothers

When You Are Discontented

Let your conversation be
without covetousness; and be
content with such things as ye
have: for he hath said, I will never
leave thee, nor forsake thee.
Hebrews 13:5 KJV

I have learned in whatever state
I am, to be content: I know how
to be abased, and I know how
to abound. Everywhere and in
all things I have learned both
to be full and to be hungry,
both to abound and to suffer need.
I can do all things through
Christ who strengthens me.
Philippians 4:11-13 NKJV

He who dwells in the shelter
of the Most High will rest in
the shadow of the Almighty.
Psalm 91:1

for Mothers

Words for the Discontent

And we know that all things work
together for good to them that love
God, to them who are the called
according to his purpose.
Romans 8:28 KJV

Those who live according to the
sinful nature have their minds set
on what that nature desires; but
those who live in accordance with
the Spirit have their minds set on
what the Spirit desires. The mind
of sinful man is death, but the
mind controlled by the
Spirit is life and peace.
Romans 8:5-6

Not that we are sufficient
of our selves to think
any thing as of ourselves;
but our sufficiency is of God.
2 Corinthians 3:5 KJV

for Mothers

The Truth about Discouragement

Why are you downcast,
O my soul? Why so disturbed
within me? Put your hope in God,
for I will yet praise him,
my Savior and my God.
Psalm 43:5

When I remember these things,
I pour out my soul within me. For
I used to go with the multitude;
I went with them to the house
of God, with the voice of joy
and praise, with a multitude
that kept a pilgrim feast.
Psalm 42:4 NKJV

Behold, the Lord thy God hath set
the land before thee: go up and
possess it, as the Lord God of
thy fathers hath said unto thee;
fear not, neither be discouraged.
Deuteronomy 1:21 KJV

for Mothers

What To Do about Discouragement

But you, be strong and
do not let your hands be weak,
for your work shall be rewarded!
2 Chronicles 15:7 NKJV

Keep your eyes open for
spiritual danger; stand true to
the Lord; act like men; be strong;
and whatever you do, do it
with kindness and love.
1 Corinthians 16:13 TLB

But Christ, God's faithful Son,
is in complete charge of God's
house. And we Christians are God's
house—he lives in us!—if we keep
up our courage firm to the end, and
our joy and our trust in the Lord.
Hebrews 3:6 TLB

Displacing Discouragement

Being confident of this very thing,
that he which hath begun a good
work in you will perform it until
the day of Jesus Christ.
Philippians 1:6 KJV

Such confidence as this is
ours through Christ before God.
Not that we are competent in
ourselves to claim anything for
ourselves, but our competence
comes from God.
2 Corinthians 3:4-5

And so, dear brothers,
now we may walk right into the
very Holy of Holies where God is,
because of the blood of Jesus.
Hebrews 10:19 TLB

for Mothers

The Truth about Encouragement

In the day when I cried thou
answeredst me, and strengthenedst
me with strength in my soul.
Though I walk in the midst of
trouble, thou wilt revive me.
Psalm 138:3,7 KJV

But from everlasting to everlasting
the Lord's love is with those
who fear him, and his
righteousness with their
children's children—with
those who keep his covenant and
remember to obey his precepts.
Psalm 103:17-18

Be strong and of good courage,
do not fear nor be afraid of them;
for the Lord your God, He is the
One who goes with you. He will
not leave you nor forsake you.
Deuteronomy 31:6 NKJV

for Mothers

How To Receive Encouragement

Be strong and of a good courage;
be not afraid, neither be
thou dismayed: for the
Lord thy God is with thee
whithersoever thou goest.
Joshua 1:9 KJV

Trust in the Lord instead. Be kind
and good to others; then you
will live safely here in the land
and prosper, feeding in safety.
Be delighted with the Lord.
Then he will give you all
your heart's desires.
Psalm 37:3-4 TLB

The humble shall see their God
at work for them . . . All who
seek for God shall live in joy.
Psalm 69:32 TLB

God's Little Book of Promises

for Mothers

How To Encourage

But exhort one another daily,
while it is called "Today," lest
any of you be hardened through
the deceitfulness of sin.
Hebrews 3:13 NKJV

Now go out and
encourage your men.
2 Samuel 19:7

Judas and Silas,
who themselves were prophets,
said much to encourage and
strengthen the brothers.
Acts 15:32

Preach the word, be urgent in
season and out of season, convince,
rebuke, and exhort, be unfailing in
patience and in teaching.
2 Timothy 4:2 RSV

for Mothers

The Truth about Failure

If the Lord delights in a man's way,
he makes his steps firm; though he
stumble, he will not fall, for the
Lord upholds him with his hand.
Psalm 37:23-24

For whatever is born of God
overcomes the world. And this
is the victory that has overcome
the world—our faith.
1 John 5:4 NKJV

The steadfast love of
the Lord never ceases,
his mercies never come to an end;
they are new every morning;
great is thy faithfulness.
Lamentations 3:22 RSV

When You Have Failed

With God's help we shall do
mighty things, for he will
trample down our foes.
Psalm 60:12 TLB

If God is for us, who can be
against us? He who did not
spare his own Son, but gave
him up for us all—how will
he not also, along with him,
graciously give us all things?
Romans 8:31-32

Now thanks be to God who always
leads us in triumph in Christ, and
through us diffuses the fragrance
of His knowledge in every place.
2 Corinthians 2:14 NKJV

for Mothers

God's Promises on Failure

Lift up your eyes to the heavens,
and look upon the earth beneath:
for the heavens shall vanish away
like smoke, and the earth shall
wax old like a garment, and they
that dwell therein shall die in like
manner: but my salvation shall be
for ever, and my righteousness
shall not be abolished.
Isaiah 51:6 KJV

All have sinned and fall short of
the glory of God, being justified
freely by His grace through the
redemption that is in Christ Jesus.
Romans 3:23-24 NKJV

For a just man falleth seven times,
and riseth up again: but the
wicked shall fall into mischief.
Proverbs 24:16 KJV

The Truth about Faith

What is faith? It is the confident
assurance that something we want
is going to happen. It is the
certainty that what we hope
for is waiting for us, even though
we cannot see it up ahead.
Hebrews 11:1 TLB

So now, since we have been made
right in God's sight by faith in his
promises, we can have real peace
with him because of what Jesus
Christ our Lord has done for us.
For because of our faith, he has
brought us into this place of
highest privilege where we now
stand, and we confidently and
joyfully look forward to
actually becoming all that
God has had in mind for us to be.
Romans 5:1-2 TLB

Faith in Action

Above all, taking the shield of
faith, wherewith ye shall be
able to quench all the fiery
darts of the wicked.
Ephesians 6:16 KJV

We walk by faith, not by sight.
2 Corinthians 5:7 NKJV

If you can believe, all things are
possible to him who believes.
Mark 9:23 NKJV

For ye are all the children of
God by faith in Christ Jesus.
Galatians 3:26 KJV

God's Faithfulness

And now just as you trusted
Christ to save you, trust him,
too, for each day's problems;
live in vital union with him.
Colossians 2:6 TLB

Whither shall I go from thy spirit?
or whither shall I flee from
thy presence? If I ascend up
into heaven, thou art there:
if I make my bed in hell, behold,
thou art there. If I take the wings
of the morning, and dwell in
the uttermost parts of the sea;
even there shall thy hand lead me,
and thy right hand shall hold me.
Psalm 139:7-10 KJV

My presence shall go with thee,
and I will give thee rest.
Exodus 33:14 KJV

God's Little Book of Promises

for Mothers

The Truth about Family

A man must leave his father and
mother when he marries, so that
he can be perfectly joined to his
wife, and the two shall be one.
Ephesians 5:31 TLB

Children, obey your parents
in the Lord, for this is right.
Honor your father and mother
(which is the first commandment
with a promise).
Ephesians 6:1-2 NASB

Be very careful never to forget
what you have seen God doing
for you. May his miracles have a
deep and permanent effect upon
your lives! Tell your children
and your grandchildren about
the glorious miracles he did.
Deuteronomy 4:9 TLB

for Mothers

Family Bonds

The wife does not have authority
over her own body, but the
husband does; and likewise
also the husband does not have
authority over his own body,
but the wife does.
1 Corinthians 7:4 NASB

If anyone says, "I love God,"
yet hates his brother, he is a liar.
For anyone who does not love his
brother, whom he has seen, cannot
love God, whom he has not seen.
And he has given us this
command: Whoever loves
God must also love his brother.
1 John 4:20-21

But if anyone does not provide
for his own, and especially
for those of his household,
he has denied the faith
and is worse than an unbeliever.
1 Timothy 5:8 NASB

for Mothers

The Family of God

Honor all people,
love the brotherhood, fear God,
honor the king.
1 Peter 2:17 NASB

Behold, how good and
how pleasant it is for brothers
to dwell together in unity!
Psalm 133:1 NASB

Truly I say to you, to the extent
that you did it to one of these
brothers of Mine, even the least
of them, you did it to Me.
Matthew 25:40 NASB

Both the one who makes men holy
and those who are made holy are
of the same family. So Jesus is not
ashamed to call them brothers.
Hebrews 2:11

The Truth about Favor

For surely, O Lord, you bless the
righteous; you surround them with
your favor as with a shield.
Psalm 5:12

A good name is to be chosen
rather than great riches, loving
favor rather than silver and gold.
Proverbs 22:1 NKJV

They did not conquer by
their own strength and skill,
but by your mighty power
and because you smiled upon
them and favored them.
Psalm 44:3 TLB

For whoever finds me finds life
and wins approval from the Lord.
Proverbs 8:35 TLB

How To Find Favor

Never tire of loyalty and kindness.
Hold these virtues tightly. Write
them deep within your heart. If
you want favor with both God and
man, and a reputation for good
judgment and common sense, then
trust the Lord completely; don't
ever trust yourself. In everything
you do, put God first and he
will direct you and crown
your efforts with success.
Proverbs 3:3-6 TLB

The Lord sets prisoners free,
the Lord gives sight to the blind,
the Lord lifts up those
who are bowed down,
the Lord loves the righteous.
Psalm 146:7-8

God's Favor

And Jesus grew in wisdom
and stature, and in favor
with God and men.
Luke 2:52

Now when he was in affliction,
he implored the Lord his God,
and humbled himself greatly
before the God of his fathers.
2 Chronicles 33:12 NKJV

But God was with him and
delivered him out of all his
troubles, and gave him favor
and wisdom in the presence of
Pharaoh, king of Egypt;
and he made him governor
over Egypt and all his house.
Acts 7:9-10 NKJV

The Truth about Fear

Fear thou not; for I am with thee:
be not dismayed; for I am thy
God: I will strengthen thee; yea,
I will help thee; yea, I will uphold
thee with the right hand
of my righteousness.
Isaiah 41:10 KJV

For God did not give us a spirit
of timidity, but a spirit of power,
of love and of self-discipline.
2 Timothy 1:7

Peace I leave with you; my peace
I give you. I do not give to you
as the world gives. Do not let
your hearts be troubled and
do not be afraid.
John 14:27

What To Do about Fear

Be anxious for nothing . . . let your
requests be made known to God;
and the peace of God, which
surpasses all understanding, will
guard your hearts and minds
through Christ Jesus.
Philippians 4:6-7 NKJV

But when I am afraid,
I will put my confidence in you.
Yes, I will trust the promises of
God. And since I am trusting him,
what can mere man do to me?
Psalm 56:3-4 TLB

Be not afraid of sudden fear, neither
of the desolation of the wicked,
when it cometh. For the Lord shall
be thy confidence, and shall keep
thy foot from being taken.
Proverbs 3:25-26 KJV

for Mothers

Strength To Replace Fear

When you go through deep
waters and great trouble,
I will be with you. When you go
through rivers of difficulty, you
will not drown! When you walk
through the fire of oppression,
you will not be burned up—
the flames will not consume you.
Isaiah 43:2 TLB

Yea, though I walk through the
valley of the shadow of death,
I will fear no evil; for You are
with me; Your rod and Your staff,
they comfort me.
Psalm 23:4 NKJV

The Lord is my light and my
salvation; whom shall I fear?
The Lord is the strength of my life;
of whom shall I be afraid?
Psalm 27:1 NKJV

God's Little Book of Promises
for Mothers

The Truth about Forgiveness

If we confess our sins, He is
faithful and just to forgive us
our sins and to cleanse us
from all unrighteousness.
1 John 1:9 NKJV

In him we have redemption
through his blood, the forgiveness
of our trespasses, according to
the riches of his grace which
he lavished upon us.
Ephesians 1:7-8 RSV

As far as the east is from the west,
so far has he removed our
transgressions from us.
Psalm 103:12

for Mothers

Receiving Forgiveness

If My people who are called by
My name will humble themselves,
and pray and seek My face,
and turn from their wicked ways,
then I will hear from heaven,
and will forgive their sin
and heal their land.
2 Chronicles 7:14 NKJV

Then I acknowledged my sin
to you and did not cover up my
iniquity. I said, "I will confess my
transgressions to the Lord"—and
you forgave the guilt of my sin.
Psalm 32:5

Your heavenly Father will
forgive you if you forgive
those who sin against you.
Matthew 6:14 TLB

Forgiving

But I say: Love your enemies! Pray
for those who persecute you! In
that way you will be acting as true
sons of your Father in heaven. For
he gives his sunlight to both the
evil and the good, and sends rain
on the just and on the unjust too.
Matthew 5:44-45 TLB

Whenever you stand praying,
forgive, if you have anything
against anyone, so that your Father
who is in heaven will also forgive
you your transgressions.
Mark 11:25-26 NASB

But love your enemies, do good,
and lend, hoping for nothing in
return. . . . Therefore be merciful,
just as your Father also is merciful.
Luke 6:35-36 NKJV

The Truth about Friendship

Two are better than one;
because they have a good reward
for their labour. For if they fall,
the one will lift up his fellow.
Ecclesiastes 4:9-10 KJV

A friend loves at all times,
and a brother is born for adversity.
Proverbs 17:17 NASB

Faithful are the wounds
of a friend, but deceitful are
the kisses of an enemy.
Proverbs 27:6 NASB

There are friends who pretend
to be friends, but there is a friend
who sticks closer than a brother.
Proverbs 18:24 RSV

Treatment of Friends

Share each other's troubles
and problems, and so obey
our Lord's command.
Galatians 6:2 TLB

But whoever loves his fellow man
is "walking in the light" and can
see his way without stumbling
around in darkness and sin.
1 John 2:10 TLB

Your friend, and your father's
friend, do not forsake.
Proverbs 27:10 RSV

Greater love has no one than this,
than to lay down one's life
for his friends.
John 15:13 NKJV

for Mothers

Fair-Weather Friends

Unfaithful creatures!
Do you not know that friendship
with the world is enmity with
God? Therefore whoever wishes to
be a friend of the world makes
himself an enemy of God.
James 4:4 RSV

He who covers over
an offense promotes love,
but whoever repeats
the matter separates close friends.
Proverbs 17:9

A perverse man sows strife,
and a whisperer separates
the best of friends.
Proverbs 16:28 NKJV

✑

The Truth about Gossip

Don't gossip. Don't falsely accuse
your neighbor of some crime,
for I am Jehovah.
Leviticus 19:16 TLB

The words of a whisperer are like
dainty morsels, and they go
down into the innermost
parts of the body.
Proverbs 18:8 NASB

Don't tell your secrets to
a gossip unless you want them
broadcast to the world.
Proverbs 20:19 TLB

Effects of Gossip

An evil man sows strife;
gossip separates the best of friends.
Proverbs 16:28 TLB

A gossip betrays a confidence,
but a trustworthy man
keeps a secret.
Proverbs 11:13

Where there is no wood,
the fire goes out; and where there
is no talebearer, strife ceases.
Proverbs 26:20 NKJV

Their throat is an open tomb;
with their tongues they have
practiced deceit; the poison of asps
is under their lips.
Romans 3:13 NKJV

Godly Speech

Let no corrupt communication
proceed out of your mouth,
but that which is good to the use
of edifying, that it may minister
grace unto the hearers.
Ephesians 4:29 KJV

Let the words of my mouth, and
the meditation of my heart,
be acceptable in thy sight, O Lord,
my strength, and my redeemer.
Psalm 19:14 KJV

Set a guard over my mouth,
O Lord; keep watch over the door
of my lips. Let not my heart
be drawn to what is evil.
Psalm 141:3-4

The Truth about Guidance

For this God is our God
for ever and ever; he will be
our guide even to the end.
Psalm 48:14

A man's heart deviseth his way:
but the Lord directeth his steps.
Proverbs 16:9 KJV

The steps of a good man
are ordered by the Lord:
and he delighteth in his way.
Psalm 37:23 KJV

I will instruct you (says the Lord)
and guide you along the best
pathway for your life; I will advise
you and watch your progress.
Psalm 32:8 TLB

❧

Guided by God

Then he led forth his people like
sheep, and guided them in the
wilderness like a flock.
Psalm 78:52 RSV

For all who are led by the Spirit
of God are sons of God.
Romans 8:14 RSV

O Lord, you are my light!
You make my darkness bright.
2 Samuel 22:29 TLB

He makes me lie down in green
pastures, he leads me beside
quiet waters, he restores my soul.
He guides me in paths of
righteousness for his name's sake.
Psalm 23:2-3

for Mothers

Being Guided

And the Lord will guide you
continually, and satisfy your desire
with good things, and make your
bones strong; and you shall be like
a watered garden, like a spring of
water, whose waters fail not.
Isaiah 58:11 RSV

When the Holy Spirit,
who is truth, comes, he shall
guide you into all truth,
for he will not be presenting
his own ideas, but will be passing
on to you what he has heard.
He will tell you about the future.
John 16:13 TLB

Call unto me, and I will
answer thee, and shew thee
great and mighty things,
which thou knowest not.
Jeremiah 33:3 KJV

The Truth about Guilt

But if we confess our sins to him,
he can be depended on to forgive
us and to cleanse us from every
wrong. [And it is perfectly
proper for God to do this
for us because Christ died
to wash away our sins.]
1 John 1:9 TLB

For I will be merciful toward their
iniquities, and I will remember
their sins no more.
Hebrews 8:12 RSV

And I will cleanse away all
their sins against me,
and pardon them.
Jeremiah 33:8 TLB

Your iniquity is taken away,
and your sin purged.
Isaiah 6:7 NKJV

Proper Guilt

When he comes, he will convict
the world of guilt in regard to sin
and righteousness and judgment.
John 16:8

Behold, the Lord comes with ten
thousands of His saints, to execute
judgment on all, to convict all
who are ungodly among them of
all their ungodly deeds which they
have committed in an ungodly
way, and of all the harsh things
which ungodly sinners have
spoken against Him.
Jude 14-15 NKJV

For God will bring every deed into
judgment, with every secret thing,
whether good or evil.
Ecclesiastes 12:14 RSV

for Mothers

When You Feel Guilt

For the Lord your God is gracious
and compassionate, and will not
turn His face away from you
if you return to Him.
2 Chronicles 30:9 NASB

He has removed our sins
as far away from us as
the east is from the west.
Psalm 103:12 TLB

And I will cleanse away all their
sins against me, and pardon them.
Jeremiah 33:8 TLB

I write to you, little children,
because your sins are forgiven
you for His name's sake.
1 John 2:12 NKJV

for Mothers

The Truth about Happiness

For to the man who pleases him
God gives wisdom and
knowledge and joy.
Ecclesiastes 2:26 RSV

A glad heart makes a cheerful
countenance, but by sorrow of
heart the spirit is broken.
Proverbs 15:13 RSV

Happiness or sadness or wealth
should not keep anyone
from doing God's work.
1 Corinthians 7:30 TLB

Happy is the man that findeth
wisdom, and the man
that getteth understanding.
Proverbs 3:13 KJV

A Time for Happiness

Is any one among you suffering?
Let him pray. Is any cheerful?
Let him sing praise.
James 5:13 RSV

And those who have reason
to be thankful should continually
be singing praises to the Lord.
James 5:13 TLB

I will bless the Lord at all times;
His praise shall continually
be in my mouth.
Psalm 34:1 NKJV

Songs of Happiness

Rejoice in the Lord always.
I will say it again: Rejoice!
Philippians 4:4

For God is the King of all
the earth; sing to him
a psalm of praise.
Psalm 47:7

I will praise you with music,
telling of your faithfulness to all
your promises, O Holy One of
Israel. I will shout and sing your
praises for redeeming me. I will
talk to others all day long about
your justice and your goodness.
Psalm 71:22-24 TLB

The Truth about
Health and Healing

Yes, I will bless the Lord and not
forget the glorious things he does
for me. He forgives all my sins.
He heals me.
Psalm 103:2-3 TLB

Surely He has borne our griefs
and carried our sorrows; yet we
esteemed Him stricken, smitten
by God, and afflicted. But He was
wounded for our transgressions,
He was bruised for our iniquities;
the chastisement for our peace
was upon Him, and by
His stripes we are healed.
Isaiah 53:4-5 NKJV

And ye shall serve the Lord your
God, and he shall bless thy bread,
and thy water; and I will take
sickness away from the midst of thee.
Exodus 23:25 KJV

❧

Jesus and Healing

And all the crowd sought to touch
him, for power came forth from
him and healed them all.
Luke 6:19 RSV

Jesus went throughout Galilee,
teaching in their synagogues,
preaching the good news
of the kingdom, and healing
every disease and sickness
among the people.
Matthew 4:23

Look! A leper is approaching.
He kneels before him, worshiping.
"Sir," the leper pleads, "if you want
to, you can heal me." Jesus touches
the man. "I want to," he says.
"Be healed." And instantly the
leprosy disappears.
Matthew 8:2-3 TLB

for Mothers

Believers and Healing

Is anyone among you sick?
Let him call for the elders of
the church, and let them pray
over him, anointing him with oil
in the name of the Lord. And the
prayer of faith will save the sick,
and the Lord will raise him up.
And if he has committed sins,
he will be forgiven.
James 5:14-15 NKJV

Heal the sick, raise the dead,
cleanse lepers, cast out demons.
Matthew 10:8 RSV

Little children, you are of God,
and have overcome them;
for he who is in you is greater
than he who is in the world.
1 John 4:4 RSV

❦

The Truth about Hope

Behold, the eye of the Lord is
upon them that fear him, upon
them that hope in his mercy.
Psalm 33:18 KJV

It is good that a man should both
hope and quietly wait for the
salvation of the Lord.
Lamentations 3:26 KJV

Happy is he whose help is
the God of Jacob, whose hope is
in the Lord his God.
Psalm 146:5 RSV

Through him we have obtained
access to this grace in which we
stand, and we rejoice in our hope
of sharing the glory of God.
Romans 5:2 RSV

Looking for Hope

Praise be to the God and Father of
our Lord Jesus Christ! In his great
mercy he has given us new birth
into a living hope through the
resurrection of Jesus Christ from
the dead, and into an inheritance
that can never perish, spoil or
fade—kept in heaven for you.
1 Peter 1:3

O Lord, you alone are my hope;
I've trusted you from childhood.
Psalm 71:5 TLB

May those who fear you rejoice
when they see me, for I have
put my hope in your word.
Psalm 119:74

When You Need Hope

But O my soul, don't be
discouraged. Don't be upset.
Expect God to act! For I know that
I shall again have plenty of reason
to praise him for all that he will
do. He is my help! He is my God!
Psalm 42:11 TLB

Be of good courage, and he
shall strengthen your heart,
all ye that hope in the Lord.
Psalm 31:24 KJV

Put your hope in God,
for I will yet praise him,
my Savior and my God.
Psalm 42:5

for Mothers

The Truth about Hospitality

Cheerfully share your home
with those who need a meal
or a place to stay for the night.
God has given each of you
some special abilities; be sure
to use them to help each other.
1 Peter 4:9-10 TLB

I tell you the truth, anyone who
gives you a cup of water in my
name because you belong to Christ
will certainly not lose his reward.
Mark 9:41

In all things I have shown you that
by so toiling one must help the
weak, remembering the words
of the Lord Jesus, how he said,
"It is more blessed to
give than to receive."
Acts 20:35 RSV

for Mothers

Who Needs Hospitality

When God's children are in need,
you be the one to help them out.
And get into the habit of inviting
guests home for dinner or, if they
need lodging, for the night.
Romans 12:13 TLB

Don't forget to be kind to
strangers, for some who have
done this have entertained
angels without realizing it!
Hebrews 13:2 TLB

Be hospitable to one another
without grumbling.
1 Peter 4:9 NKJV

We ought therefore to show
hospitality to such men so that we
may work together for the truth.
3 John 8

How To Show Hospitality

For I was hungry, and you gave
Me something to eat; I was thirsty,
and you gave Me something to
drink; I was a stranger, and you
invited Me in; naked, and you
clothed Me; I was sick, and you
visited Me; I was in prison,
and you came to Me.
Matthew 25:35-36 NASB

The King will answer and say to
them, "Truly I say to you, to the
extent that you did it to one of
these brothers of Mine, even the
least of them, you did it to Me."
Matthew 25:40 NASB

Dear children, let us not love
with words or tongue but
with actions and in truth.
1 John 3:18

The Truth about Injustice

Happy are those who are
persecuted because they are good,
for the Kingdom of Heaven is
theirs. When you are reviled and
persecuted and lied about because
you are my followers—wonderful!
Be happy about it! Be very glad!
For a tremendous reward awaits
you up in heaven. And remember,
the ancient prophets were
persecuted too.
Matthew 5:10-12 TLB

Many are the afflictions of
the righteous: but the Lord
delivereth him out of them all.
Psalm 34:19 KJV

Do not be surprised, my brothers,
if the world hates you.
1 John 3:13

❦

Righteous Justice

He is the Rock, his work is perfect:
for all his ways are judgment:
a God of truth and without
iniquity, just and right is he.
Deuteronomy 32:4 KJV

Yet ye say, The way of the Lord is
not equal. Hear now, O house of
Israel; is not my way equal?
are not your ways unequal?
Ezekiel 18:25 KJV

Great in counsel and mighty
in deed; whose eyes are open to
all the ways of men, rewarding
every man according to
his ways and according
to the fruit of his doings.
Jeremiah 32:19 RSV

Bearing Injustice—
A Call To Action

Defend the poor and fatherless; do
justice to the afflicted and needy.
Deliver the poor and needy; free
them from the hand of the wicked.
Psalm 82:3-4 NKJV

She opens her arms to
the poor and extends
her hands to the needy.
Proverbs 31:20

He has shown you, O man,
what is good; and what does
the Lord require of you but to
do justly, to love mercy, and to
walk humbly with your God?
Micah 6:8 NKJV

The Truth about Jealousy

For where you have envy and
selfish ambition, there you find
disorder and every evil practice.
James 3:16

Be still before the Lord and wait
patiently for him; do not fret when
men succeed in their ways,
when they carry out their
wicked schemes.
Psalm 37:7

If we live by the Spirit, let us also
walk by the Spirit. Let us have no
self-conceit, no provoking of one
another, no envy of one another.
Galatians 5:25-26 RSV

You shall not covet.
Exodus 20:17 NKJV

Jealousy's Wreckage

For the wicked boasteth of his
heart's desire, and blesseth
the covetous, whom the
Lord abhorreth.
Psalm 10:3 KJV

Wrath is cruel, anger is
overwhelming; but who
can stand before jealously?
Proverbs 27:4 RSV

Do not envy wicked men,
do not desire their company;
for their hearts plot violence,
and their lips talk about
making trouble.
Proverbs 24:1-2

But if you harbor bitter envy and
selfish ambition in your hearts,
do not boast about it.
James 3:14

Righteous Jealousy

Do you think that the Scripture
says in vain, "The Spirit who
dwells in us yearns jealously"?
James 4:5 NKJV

You shall not make for yourself an
idol in the form of anything in
heaven above or on the earth
beneath or in the waters below.
You shall not bow down to them
or worship them; for I, the Lord
your God, am a jealous God.
Exodus 20:4-5

Be careful not to forget the
covenant of the Lord your God . . .
do not make for yourselves an
idol . . . For the Lord your God
is a consuming fire, a jealous God.
Deuteronomy 4:23-24

The Truth about Joy

For you shall go out in joy, and be
led forth in peace; the mountains
and the hills before you shall break
forth into singing, and all the trees
of the field shall clap their hands.
Isaiah 55:12 RSV

And the ransomed of the Lord
shall return, and come to Zion
with singing; everlasting joy shall
be upon their heads; they shall
obtain joy and gladness, and
sorrow and sighing shall flee away.
Isaiah 51:11 RSV

Then he said to them, "Go your
way . . . for this day is holy to our
Lord; and do not be grieved, for the
joy of the Lord is your strength."
Nehemiah 8:10 RSV

Joy in God

No wonder we are happy in the
Lord! For we are trusting him.
We trust his holy name.
Psalm 33:21 TLB

I will greatly rejoice in the Lord,
my soul shall exult in my God;
for he has clothed me with the
garments of salvation, he has
covered me with the robe of
righteousness, as the bridegroom
decks himself with a garland,
and as a bride adorns herself
with her jewels.
Isaiah 61:10 RSV

My soul is feasted as with
marrow and fat, and my mouth
praises thee with joyful lips,
when I think of thee upon my bed,
and meditate on thee in the
watches of the night.
Psalm 63:5 RSV

for Mothers

Joyful, Joyful

Yes, the gladness you have given
me is far greater than their joys
at harvest time as they gaze
at their bountiful crops.
Psalm 4:7 TLB

May those who sow in tears reap
with shouts of joy! He that goes
forth weeping, bearing the seed
for sowing, shall come home
with shouts of joy, bringing
his sheaves with him.
Psalm 126:5-6 RSV

So you have sorrow now,
but I will see you again
and your hearts will rejoice,
and no one will take
your joy from you.
John 16:22 RSV

for Mothers

The Truth about Justice

As for the Almighty, we cannot
find Him; He is excellent in power,
in judgment and abundant justice;
He does not oppress.
Job 37:23 NKJV

Arise, O Lord, in thy anger,
lift thyself up against the fury of
my enemies; awake, O my God;
thou hast appointed a judgment.
Psalm 7:6 RSV

But let him who glories glory
in this, that he understands and
knows me, that I am the Lord who
practice steadfast love, justice,
and righteousness in the earth;
for in these things I delight.
Jeremiah 9:24 RSV

for Mothers

God's Justice

He does not crush the weak,
or quench the smallest hope;
He will end all conflict with his
final victory, and his name shall
be the hope of all the world.
Matthew 12:20-21 TLB

God presented him as a sacrifice
of atonement, through faith in his
blood. He did this to demonstrate
his justice, because in his
forbearance he had left the sins
committed beforehand unpunished.
Romans 3:25

The Lord has made himself
known, he has executed judgment;
the wicked are snared in the work
of their own hands.
Psalm 9:16 RSV

for Mothers

Seeking Justice

Follow justice and justice alone,
so that you may live and possess
the land the Lord your
God is giving you.
Deuteronomy 16:20

The king's strength also loveth
judgment; thou dost establish
equity, thou executest judgment
and righteousness in Jacob.
Psalm 99:4 KJV

Learn to do well; seek judgment,
relieve the oppressed, judge the
fatherless, plead for the widow.
Isaiah 1:17 KJV

But let justice roll down like
waters, and righteousness like
an everflowing stream.
Amos 5:24 RSV

God's Little Book of Promises
for Mothers

The Truth about Loneliness

Behold, I am with you and will
keep you wherever you go,
and will bring you back to this
land; for I will not leave you
until I have done that of which
I have spoken to you.
Genesis 28:15 RSV

All those who know your mercy,
Lord, will count on you for help.
For you have never yet forsaken
those who trust in you.
Psalm 9:10 TLB

I will never, never fail you
nor forsake you.
Hebrews 13:5 TLB

God sets the lonely in families,
he leads forth the prisoners
with singing.
Psalm 68:6

When You Are Lonely

The eternal God is thy refuge, and
underneath are the everlasting arms.
Deuteronomy 33:27 KJV

Who shall separate us from the
love of Christ? Shall tribulation, or
distress, or perscution, or famine,
or nakedness, or peril, or sword?
Yet in all these things we are more
than conquerors through Him who
loved us. For I am persuaded that
neither death nor life, nor angels
nor principalities nor powers, nor
things present nor things to come,
nor height nor depth, nor any
other created thing, shall
be able to separate us from
the love of God which
is in Christ Jesus our Lord.
Romans 8:35,37-39 NKJV

Solitude Replaces Loneliness

Be still, and know that I am God;
I will be exalted among the nations,
I will be exalted in the earth.
Psalm 46:10

Early in the morning,
before the sun is up, I was praying
and pointing out how much
I trust in you. I stay awake
through the night to
think about your promises.
Psalm 119:147-148 TLB

You are my hiding place from
every storm of life; you even keep
me from getting into trouble! You
surround me with songs of victory.
Psalm 32:7 TLB

The Truth about Loss

And God will wipe away every tear
from their eyes; there shall
be no more death, nor sorrow,
nor crying. There shall
be no more pain.
Revelation 21:4 NKJV

Weeping may remain for a night,
but rejoicing comes
in the morning.
Psalm 30:5

He heals the brokenhearted and
binds up their wounds.
Psalm 147:3 NKJV

There is a time for everything,
and a season for every activity
under heaven: a time to mourn
and a time to dance.
Ecclesiastes 3:1,4

❧

Strength for Loss

To all who mourn in Israel
he will give: Beauty for ashes;
joy instead of mourning;
praise instead of heaviness.
Isaiah 61:3 TLB

Blessed are those who mourn,
for they will be comforted.
Matthew 5:4

Shout for joy, O heavens;
rejoice, O earth; burst into song,
O mountains! For the Lord
comforts his people and will have
compassion on his afflicted ones.
Isaiah 49:13

For as the sufferings of Christ
abound in us, so our consolation
also abounds through Christ.
2 Corinthians 1:5 NKJV

❧

Comforting Loss

Rejoice with those who rejoice;
mourn with those who mourn.
Romans 12:15

Therefore, as the elect of God,
holy and beloved, put on tender
mercies, kindness, humility,
meekness, longsuffering.
Colossians 3:12 NKJV

Blessed be the God and Father of
our Lord Jesus Christ, the Father
of mercies and God of all comfort,
who comforts us in all our
tribulation, that we may be able
to comfort those who are in
any trouble, with the comfort
with which we ourselves
are comforted by God.
2 Corinthians 1:3-4 NKJV

The Truth about Love

And now these three remain:
faith, hope and love.
But the greatest of these is love.
1 Corinthians 13:13

Work instead at what is right
and good, learning to
trust him and love others,
and to be patient and gentle.
1 Timothy 6:11 TLB

And above all things have fervent
love for one another, for "love will
cover a multitude of sins."
1 Peter 4:8 NKJV

And above all these put on love,
which binds everything together
in perfect harmony.
Colossians 3:14 RSV

for Mothers

Love between God and People

For God so loved the world that
he gave his only Son, that whoever
believes in him should not
perish but have eternal life.
John 3:16 RSV

And he will love thee,
and bless thee, and multiply thee.
Deuteronomy 7:13 KJV

The Lord sets prisoners free,
the Lord gives sight to
the blind, the Lord lifts up
those who are bowed down,
the Lord loves the righteous.
Psalm 146:7-8

The Lord your God is with you, he
is mighty to save. He will take
great delight in you, he will quiet
you with his love, he will rejoice
over you with singing.
Zephaniah 3:17

for Mothers

Love between Us

Love your neighbor as yourself:
I am the Lord.
Leviticus 19:18 NKJV

For the whole Law can be summed
up in this one command:
"Love others as you love yourself."
Galatians 5:14 TLB

By this all men will know that
you are my disciples, if you
have love for one another.
John 13:35 RSV

Beloved, let us love one another;
for love is of God, and he who
loves is born of God and knows
God. He who does not love does
not know God; for God is love.
1 John 4:7-8 RSV

The Truth about Marriage

And the Lord God said,
It is not good that the man
should be alone; I will make
him an help meet for him.
Genesis 2:18 KJV

Therefore what God has joined
together, let man not separate.
Matthew 19:6

He who finds a wife
finds a good thing, and
obtains favor from the Lord.
Proverbs 18:22 NKJV

Marriage should be honored by all,
and the marriage bed kept pure,
for God will judge the adulterer
and all the sexually immoral.
Hebrews 13:4

Husband and Wife

Therefore a man leaves his father
and his mother and cleaves to his
wife, and they become one flesh.
Genesis 2:24 RSV

A wife of noble character who
can find? She is worth far more
than rubies. Her husband has
full confidence in her and lacks
nothing of value. Her children
arise and call her blessed; her
husband also, and he praises her.
Proverbs 31:10-11,28

For the husband is the head
of the wife, even as Christ
is the head of the church:
and he is the saviour of the body.
Ephesians 5:23 KJV

for Mothers

Marriage of Souls

Wives, fit in with your husbands'
plans; for then if they refuse to
listen when you talk to them about
the Lord, they will be won by
your respectful, pure behavior.
Your godly lives will speak to
them better than any words.
1 Peter 3:1-2 TLB

For the unbelieving husband is
consecrated through his wife,
and the unbelieving wife is
consecrated through her husband.
1 Corinthians 7:14 RSV

You wives, submit yourselves to
your husbands, for that is what the
Lord has planned for you. And
you husbands must be loving
and kind to your wives and not
bitter against them, nor harsh.
Colossians 3:18-19 TLB

God's Little Book of Promises

for Mothers

The Truth about Mercy

Let us therefore come boldly unto
the throne of grace, that we may
obtain mercy, and find grace to
help in time of need.
Hebrews 4:16 KJV

I will make all my goodness pass
before thee, and I will proclaim the
name of the Lord before thee; and
will be gracious to whom I will be
gracious, and will shew mercy on
whom I will shew mercy.
Exodus 33:19 KJV

Give knowledge of salvation
to his people in the forgiveness of
their sins, through the tender
mercy of our God.
Luke 1:77-78 RSV

Merciful God

The Lord is gracious, and full of
compassion; slow to anger,
and of great mercy. The Lord
is good to all: and his tender
mercies are over all his works.
Psalm 145:8-9 KJV

Who is a God like you, who
pardons sins and forgives the
transgression of the remnant of his
inheritance? You do not stay angry
forever but delight to show mercy.
Micah 7:18

Foreigners will come and build
your cities. Presidents and kings
will send you aid. For though I
destroyed you in my anger,
I will have mercy on you
through my grace.
Isaiah 60:10 TLB

When You Need Mercy

For thou, Lord, art good,
and ready to forgive;
and plenteous in mercy unto
all them that call upon thee.
Psalm 86:5 KJV

Yet the Lord still waits for you to
come to him, so he can show you
his love; he will conquer you to
bless you, just as he said. For the
Lord is faithful to his promises.
Blessed are all those who wait
for him to help them.
Isaiah 30:18 TLB

But the lovingkindness of
the Lord is from everlasting
to everlasting, to those who
reverence him; his salvation is to
children's children of those who
are faithful to his covenant and
remember to obey him!
Psalm 103:17-18 TLB

God's Little Book of Promises

for Mothers

The Truth about Obedience

To obey is better than sacrifice, and
to hearken than the fat of rams.
1 Samuel 15:22 KJV

Therefore, O Israel, listen closely
to each command and be careful
to obey it, so that all will go well
with you, and so that you will
have many children. If you obey
these commands you will become
a great nation in a glorious land
"flowing with milk and honey,"
even as the God of your
fathers promised you.
Deuteronomy 6:3 TLB

If they obey and serve him, they
will spend the rest of their days in
prosperity and their years in
contentment.
Job 36:11

God's Little Book of Promises
for Mothers

Examples of Obedience

He who has my commandments
and keeps them, he it is who loves
me; and he who loves me will be
loved by my Father, and I will love
him and manifest myself to him.
John 14:21 RSV

Because of your obedience, the
Lord your God will keep his
part of the contract which,
in his tender love,
he made with your fathers.
Deuteronomy 7:12 TLB

When you obey me you are living
in my love, just as I obey my
Father and live in his love.
John 15:10 TLB

Obedient Servants

And this world is fading away, and
these evil, forbidden things will go
with it, but whoever keeps doing
the will of God will live forever.
1 John 2:17 TLB

And how can we be sure that we
belong to him? By looking within
ourselves: are we really trying
to do what he wants us to?
1 John 2:3 TLB

But, dearly loved friends, if our
consciences are clear, we can come
to the Lord with perfect assurance
and trust, and get whatever we ask
for because we are obeying him and
doing the things that please him.
1 John 3:21-22 TLB

The Truth about Patience

You need to keep on patiently
doing God's will if you want
him to do for you all
that he has promised.
Hebrews 10:36 TLB

Dear brothers, is your life full of
difficulties and temptations?
Then be happy, for when the way
is rough, your patience has a
chance to grow. So let it grow, and
don't try to squirm out of your
problems. For when your patience
is finally in full bloom, then you
will be ready for anything, strong
in character, full and complete.
James 1:2-4 TLB

For ye have need of patience, that,
after ye have done the will of God,
ye might receive the promise.
Hebrews 10:36 KJV

Godly Patience

But You, O Lord, are a God
full of compassion, and gracious,
longsuffering and abundant
in mercy and truth.
Psalm 86:15 NKJV

The Lord is merciful and gracious,
slow to anger, and plenteous
in mercy. He will not always
chide: neither will he keep
his anger for ever.
Psalm 103:8-9 KJV

And he passed in front of Moses,
proclaiming, "The Lord, the Lord,
the compassionate and gracious
God, slow to anger, abounding in
love and faithfulness, maintaining
love to thousands, and forgiving
wickedness, rebellion and sin."
Exodus 34:6

God's Little Book of Promises

Patience, Patience

Put on a heart of compassion,
kindness, humility, gentleness and
patience; bearing with one another,
and forgiving each other, whoever
has a complaint against anyone;
just as the Lord forgave you,
so also should you.
Colossians 3:12-13 NASB

Be humble and gentle.
Be patient with each other,
making allowance for each other's
faults because of your love.
Ephesians 4:2 TLB

You will be anxious to follow
the example of those who receive
all that God has promised them
because of their strong
faith and patience.
Hebrews 6:12 TLB

The Truth about Persecution

Remember the word that I said to you, "A servant is not greater than his master." If they persecuted Me, they will also persecute you.
John 15:20 NKJV

Blessed are those who have been persecuted for the sake of righteousness, for theirs is the kingdom of heaven. Blessed are you when people insult you and persecute you, and falsely say all kinds of evil against you because of Me.
Matthew 5:10-11 NASB

Yes, and those who decide to please Christ Jesus by living godly lives will suffer at the hands of those who hate him.
2 Timothy 3:12 TLB

for Mothers

How To Handle Persecution

But we have this treasure in
earthen vessels, so that the
surpassing greatness of the power
will be of God and not from
ourselves; we are afflicted in every
way, but not crushed; perplexed,
but not despairing; persecuted, but
not forsaken; struck down, but not
destroyed; always carrying about
in the body the dying of Jesus,
so that the life of Jesus also may
be manifested in our body.
2 Corinthians 4:7-10 NASB

Who shall separate us from the
love of Christ? Shall trouble or
hardship or persecution or famine
or nakedness or danger or sword?
No, in all these things we are more
than conquerors through
him who loved us.
Romans 8:35,37

for Mothers

❧

Those Who Persecute You

I say: Love your enemies!
Pray for those who persecute you!
In that way you will be acting as
true sons of your Father in heaven.
Matthew 5:44-45 TLB

If someone mistreats you because
you are a Christian, don't curse
him; pray that God will bless him.
Romans 12:14 TLB

If your enemy is hungry, give him
food to eat; and if he is thirsty,
give him water to drink;
for you will heap burning
coals on his head, and the
Lord will reward you.
Proverbs 25:21-22 NASB

for Mothers

The Truth about Perseverance

May the Lord direct
your hearts into God's love
and Christ's perseverance.
2 Thessalonians 3:5

[Love] always protects,
always trusts, always hopes,
always perseveres.
1 Corinthians 13:7

"My grace is sufficient for you, for
my power is made perfect in
weakness." Therefore I will boast
all the more gladly about my
weaknesses, so that Christ's power
may rest on me.
2 Corinthians 12:9

◈

Perseverance under Trials

We also glory in tribulations,
knowing that tribulation produces
perseverance; and perseverance,
character; and character, hope.
Now hope does not disappoint,
because the love of God has been
poured out in our hearts by the
Holy Spirit who was given to us.
Romans 5:3-5 NKJV

Because you know that the testing
of your faith develops
perseverance. Perseverance
must finish its work so that you
may be mature and complete,
not lacking anything.
James 1:3-4

But if anyone suffers as a Christian,
he is not to be ashamed, but is to
glorify God in this name.
1 Peter 4:16 NASB

for Mothers

Perseverance Has Its Benefits

You need to persevere so
that when you have done
the will of God, you will
receive what he has promised.
Hebrews 10:36

Take heed to yourself and to the
doctrine. Continue in them,
for in doing this you will save both
yourself and those who hear you.
1 Timothy 4:16 NKJV

But the seed on good soil
stands for those with a noble and
good heart, who hear the word,
retain it, and by persevering
produce a crop.
Luke 8:15

The Truth about Protection

If you make the Most High your
dwelling—even the Lord, who is
my refuge—then no harm will
befall you, no disaster will come
near your tent. For he will
command his angels concerning
you to guard you in all your ways.
Psalm 91:9-11

No weapon forged against you will
prevail, and you will refute every
tongue that accuses you. This is
the heritage of the servants of
the Lord, and this is their
vindication from me.
Isaiah 54:17

In peace I will both lie down and
sleep; for thou alone, O Lord,
makest me dwell in safety.
Psalm 4:8 RSV

Heavenly Protection

Fear not, for I am with you, be
not dismayed, for I am your God;
I will strengthen you, I will help
you, I will uphold you with
my victorious right hand.
Isaiah 41:10 RSV

The Lord shall preserve you from
all evil; He shall preserve your soul.
The Lord shall preserve your going
out and your coming in from this
time forth, and even forevermore.
Psalm 121:7-8 NKJV

When you pass through the
waters, I will be with you; and
when you pass through the rivers,
they will not sweep over you.
When you walk through the fire,
you will not be burned;
the flames will not set you ablaze.
Isaiah 43:2

Being Protected

The angel of the Lord encamps
around those who fear him, and he
delivers them. Taste and see that
the Lord is good; blessed is the
man who takes refuge in him.
Psalm 34:7-8

The Lord is a strong fortress.
The godly run to him and are safe.
Proverbs 18:10 TLB

He does not fear bad news, nor
live in dread of what may happen.
For he is settled in his mind that
Jehovah will take care of him.
Psalm 112:7 TLB

The Truth about Reconciliation

Pursue peace with all people, and
holiness, without which no one
will see the Lord: looking carefully
lest anyone fall short of the grace of
God; lest any root of bitterness
springing up cause trouble, and
by this many become defiled.
Hebrews 12:14-15 NKJV

Blessed are the merciful:
for they shall obtain mercy.
Matthew 5:7 KJV

Do not be overcome by evil,
but overcome evil with good.
Romans 12:21

Be kind and compassionate to
one another, forgiving each other,
just as in Christ God forgave you.
Ephesians 4:32

for Mothers

When You Have Been Wronged

The discretion of a man makes
him slow to anger, and his glory is
to overlook a transgression.
Proverbs 19:11 NKJV

Do not resist an evil person. If
someone strikes you on the right
cheek, turn to him the other also.
Matthew 5:39

And whenever you stand praying,
forgive, if you have anything
against any one; so that your
Father also who is in heaven
may forgive you your trespasses.
Mark 11:25 RSV

If thy brother trespass against thee,
rebuke him; and if he repent,
forgive him.
Luke 17:3 KJV

When You Are Wrong

But love your enemies, and do good, and lend, expecting nothing in return; and your reward will be great, and you will be sons of the Most High; for he is kind to the ungrateful and the selfish.
Luke 6:35 RSV

Why do you look at the speck of sawdust in your brother's eye and pay no attention to the plank in your own eye? How can you say to your brother, "Let me take the speck out of your eye," when all the time there is a plank in your own eye? You hypocrite, first take the plank out of your own eye, and then you will see clearly to remove the speck from your brother's eye.
Matthew 7:3-5

The Truth about Rejection

Behold what manner of love the
Father has bestowed on us, that
we should be called children of
God! Therefore the world does not
know us, because it did not know
Him. Beloved, now we are
children of God; and it has not yet
been revealed what we shall be,
but we know that when He is
revealed, we shall be like Him,
for we shall see Him as He is.
1 John 3:1-2 NKJV

A man of many companions may
come to ruin, but there is a friend
who sticks closer than a brother.
Proverbs 18:24

for Mothers

Feeling Rejected

For he chose us in him before the
creation of the world to be holy
and blameless in his sight. In love
he predestined us to be adopted as
his sons through Jesus Christ,
in accordance with his pleasure
and will—to the praise of his
glorious grace, which he has freely
given us in the One he loves.
Ephesians 1:4-6

For the Lord will not forsake his
people; he will not abandon his
heritage; for justice will return to
the righteous, and all the upright
in heart will follow it.
Psalm 94:14-15 RSV

The Rejected Have Hope

The poor and needy seek water,
but there is none, their tongues
fail for thirst. I, the Lord,
will hear them; I, the God of
Israel, will not forsake them.
Isaiah 41:17 NKJV

And Jesus said, "I do not
condemn you, either. Go.
From now on sin no more."
John 8:11 NASB

He was despised and forsaken
of men, a man of sorrows and
acquainted with grief; and like
one from whom men hide their
face, He was despised, and we
did not esteem Him. Surely
our griefs He Himself bore,
and our sorrows He carried.
Isaiah 53:3-4 NASB

for Mothers

The Truth about Relationships

But if we walk in the light, as he is
in the light, we have fellowship with
one another, and the blood of Jesus,
his Son, purifies us from all sin.
1 John 1:7

And the Scripture was fulfilled
which says, "Abraham believed
God, and it was accounted to him
for righteousness." And he was
called the friend of God.
James 2:23 NKJV

My command is this: Love each
other as I have loved you. Greater
love has no one than this, that he
lay down his life for his friends.
You are my friends if you
do what I command.
John 15:12-14

for Mothers

Family Ties

Children, obey your parents in the
Lord: for this is right.
Ephesians 6:1 KJV

Only be careful, and watch
yourselves closely so that you
do not forget the things your eyes
have seen or let them slip from
your heart as long as you live.
Teach them to your children and
to their children after them.
Deuteronomy 4:9

For the wife does not rule over
her own body, but the husband
does; likewise the husband does
not rule over his own body,
but the wife does.
1 Corinthians 7:4 RSV

Godly Relationships

A friend loves at all times.
Proverbs 17:17

Do not forsake your friend
and the friend of your father.
Proverbs 27:10

Therefore if you bring your gift to
the altar, and there remember that
your brother has something against
you, leave your gift there before
the altar, and go your way. First be
reconciled to your brother, and
then come and offer your gift.
Matthew 5:23-24 NKJV

Keep on loving each
other as brothers.
Hebrews 13:1

The Truth about Renewal

And do not be conformed to this
world, but be transformed by the
renewing of your mind, that you
may prove what is that good and
acceptable and perfect will of God.
Romans 12:2 NKJV

A new heart I will give you, and
a new spirit I will put within you;
and I will take out of your flesh
the heart of stone and give you
a heart of flesh. And I will put my
spirit within you, and cause
you to walk in my statutes and be
careful to observe my ordinances.
Ezekiel 36:26-27 RSV

If we confess our sins,
he is faithful and just to forgive
us our sins, and to cleanse us
from all unrighteousness.
1 John 1:9 KJV

God's Little Book of Promises
for Mothers

Renewed by God

Create in me a clean heart,
O God; and renew
a right spirit within me.
Psalm 51:10 KJV

Therefore if any man be in Christ,
he is a new creature: old things
are passed away; behold,
all things are become new.
2 Corinthians 5:17 KJV

I will seek that which was lost, and
bring again that which was driven
away, and will bind up that which
was broken, and will strengthen
that which was sick: but I will
destroy the fat and the strong;
I will feed them with judgment.
Ezekiel 34:16 KJV

Renewed Believers

Be made new in the attitude of
your minds; and to put on the new
self, created to be like God in true
righteousness and holiness.
Ephesians 4:23-24

Forgetting what is behind and
straining toward what is ahead, I
press on toward the goal to win
the prize for which God has called
me heavenward in Christ Jesus.
Philippians 3:13-14

Do not lie to one another, since
you have put off the old man with
his deeds, and have put on the
new man who is renewed in
knowledge according to the
image of Him who created him.
Colossians 3:9-10 NKJV

The Truth about Resurrection

Jesus said to her, "I am the
resurrection and the life.
He who believes in Me, though
he may die, he shall live. And
whoever lives and believes
in Me shall never die."
John 11:25-26 NKJV

In a moment, in the twinkling
of an eye, at the last trump: for
the trumpet shall sound, and the
dead shall be raised incorruptible,
and we shall be changed.
1 Corinthians 15:52 KJV

You were also raised up
with Him through faith
in the working of God,
who raised Him from the dead.
Colossians 2:12 NASB

Christ's Resurrection

Seeing what was ahead, he spoke
of the resurrection of the Christ,
that he was not abandoned to the
grave, nor did his body see decay.
God has raised this Jesus to life,
and we are all witnesses of the fact.
Exalted to the right hand of God,
he has received from the Father
the promised Holy Spirit and
has poured out what you
now see and hear.
Acts 2:31-33

Blessed be the God and Father
of our Lord Jesus Christ, who
according to His abundant mercy
has begotten us again to a living
hope through the resurrection of
Jesus Christ from the dead, to an
inheritance incorruptible and
undefiled and that does not fade
away, reserved in heaven for you.
1 Peter 1:3-4 NKJV

Believers' Resurrection

For if we have been united
together in the likeness of His
death, certainly we also shall be in
the likeness of His resurrection.
Romans 6:5 NKJV

I want to know Christ and the
power of his resurrection and the
fellowship of sharing in his
sufferings, becoming like him in
his death, and so, somehow,
to attain to the resurrection
from the dead.
Philippians 3:10-11

As in Adam all die, so also in
Christ all will be made alive.
1 Corinthians 15:22 NASB

The Truth about Restoration

Restore to me the joy of thy
salvation, and uphold me with
a willing spirit. The sacrifice
acceptable to God is a broken
spirit; a broken and contrite heart,
O God, thou wilt not despise.
Psalm 51:12,17 RSV

Restore us, O God;
make your face shine upon us,
that we may be saved.
Psalm 80:3

Turn us back to You, O Lord,
and we will be restored;
renew our days as of old.
Lamentations 5:21 NKJV

God's Role

The Lord will restore the splendor
of Jacob like the splendor of Israel,
though destroyers have laid them
waste and have ruined their vines.
Nahum 2:2

And the God of all grace, who
called you to his eternal glory in
Christ, after you have suffered a
little while, will himself restore
you and make you strong, firm
and steadfast. To him be the
power for ever and ever. Amen.
1 Peter 5:10-11

He restores my soul.
Psalm 23:3 NKJV

Our Role

Repent, and let every one of you
be baptized in the name of Jesus
Christ for the remission of sins;
and you shall receive the
gift of the Holy Spirit.
Acts 2:38 NKJV

Cast away from you all your
transgressions, whereby ye have
transgressed; and make you a
new heart and a new spirit.
Ezekiel 18:31 KJV

Repent ye therefore, and be
converted, that your sins may be
blotted out, when the times of
refreshing shall come from
the presence of the Lord.
Acts 3:19 KJV

The Truth about Self-Worth

For You formed my inward parts;
You covered me in my mother's
womb. I will praise You, for I am
fearfully and wonderfully made;
marvelous are Your works, and
that my soul knows very well.
Psalm 139:13-14 NKJV

Put on the new self, which in
the likeness of God has been
created in righteousness and
holiness of the truth.
Ephesians 4:24 NASB

For I know the thoughts that I
think toward you, saith the Lord,
thoughts of peace, and not of evil,
to give you an expected end.
Jeremiah 29:11 KJV

Finding Worth

And since we are his children,
we will share his treasures—
for all God gives to his Son
Jesus is now ours too.
Romans 8:17 TLB

How great is the love the Father
has lavished on us, that we should
be called children of God!
1 John 3:1

He chose us in Him before the
foundation of the world, that
we should be holy and without
blame before Him in love, having
predestined us to adoption as
sons by Jesus Christ to Himself,
according to the good pleasure of
His will, to the praise of the glory
of His grace, by which He made
us accepted in the Beloved.
Ephesians 1:4-6 NKJV

Worth in Our Calling

I have loved you with an
everlasting love; therefore with
loving-kindness have I drawn you.
Jeremiah 31:3 AMP

We have not received the spirit of
the world but the Spirit who is
from God, that we may understand
what God has freely given us.
1 Corinthians 2:12

That Christ may dwell in your
hearts through faith; that you,
being rooted and grounded in
love, may be able to comprehend
with all the saints what is the
width and length and depth
and height—to know the love of
Christ which passes knowledge;
that you may be filled with
all the fullness of God.
Ephesians 3:17-19 NKJV

The Truth about Shame

Fear not; you will no longer
live in shame.
Isaiah 54:4 TLB

Indeed, let no one who
waits on You be ashamed;
let those be ashamed who deal
treacherously without cause.
Psalm 25:3 NKJV

May those who hope in you not be
disgraced because of me, O Lord,
the Lord Almighty; may those who
seek you not be put to shame.
Psalm 69:6

Behold, I lay in Zion a stumbling
stone and rock of offense,
and whoever believes on Him
will not be put to shame.
Romans 9:33 NKJV

❦

Hope for Shame

Then, when that happens, we are
able to hold our heads high no
matter what happens and know
that all is well, for we know how
dearly God loves us, and we feel
this warm love everywhere within
us because God has given us the
Holy Spirit to fill our hearts
with his love.
Romans 5:5 TLB

Therefore being justified by faith,
we have peace with God through
our Lord Jesus Christ.
Romans 5:1 KJV

There is now no condemnation for
those who are in Christ Jesus.
Romans 8:1 NASB

Not Ashamed

But if anyone suffers as a
Christian, he is not to be ashamed,
but is to glorify God in this name.
1 Peter 4:16 NASB

For I am not ashamed of the
gospel of Christ, for it is the
power of God to salvation for
everyone who believes.
Romans 1:16 NKJV

So do not be ashamed
to testify about our Lord.
2 Timothy 1:8

Be diligent to present yourself
approved to God, a worker who
does not need to be ashamed,
rightly dividing the word of truth.
2 Timothy 2:15 NKJV

for Mothers

The Truth about Stewardship

He who is faithful in what is least
is faithful also in much; and he
who is unjust in what is least is
unjust also in much.
Luke 16:10 NKJV

Now it is required that those
who have been given a trust
must prove faithful.
1 Corinthians 4:2

As each one has received a gift,
minister it to one another,
as good stewards of the
manifold grace of God.
1 Peter 4:10 NKJV

Good will come to him who is
generous and lends freely, who
conducts his affairs with justice.
Psalm 112:5

God's Stewards

Moreover it is required in stewards
that one be found faithful.
1 Corinthians 4:2 NKJV

And he sat down opposite the
treasury, and watched the
multitude putting money into the
treasury. Many rich people put in
large sums. And a poor widow
came, and put in two copper
coins, which make a penny. And
he called his disciples to him, and
said to them, "Truly, I say to you,
this poor widow has put in more
that all those who are contributing
to the treasury. For they
all contributed out of their
abundance; but she out of her
poverty has put in everything
she had, her whole living."
Mark 12:41-44 RSV

How To Be Stewardly

So when you give to the needy,
do not announce it with trumpets,
as the hypocrites do in the
synagogues and on the streets,
to be honored by men. I tell you
the truth, they have received their
reward in full. But when you give
to the needy, do not let your left
hand know what your right
hand is doing, so that your
giving may be in secret.
Matthew 6:2-4

Command those who are rich in
this present age not to be haughty,
nor to trust in uncertain riches but
in the living God, who gives us
richly all things to enjoy. Let them
do good, that they be rich in
good works, ready to give,
willing to share.
1 Timothy 6:17-18 NKJV

The Truth about Strength

The Lord is my strength and song,
and he is become my salvation:
he is my God, and I will prepare
him an habitation; my father's
God, and I will exalt him.
Exodus 15:2 KJV

He will give his people strength.
He will bless them with peace.
Psalm 29:11 TLB

My grace is sufficient for you,
for My strength is made
perfect in weakness.
2 Corinthians 12:9 NKJV

Finally, my brethren,
be strong in the Lord,
and in the power of his might.
Ephesians 6:10 KJV

❧

Women of Strength

But the angel said to her, "Do not
be afraid, Mary, you have found
favor with God. You will be with
child and give birth to a son, and
you are to give him the name
Jesus." "I am the Lord's servant,"
Mary answered. "May it be to
me as you have said."
Luke 1:30-31,38

Strength and honor are her
clothing; she shall rejoice in time
to come. She opens her mouth
with wisdom, and on her tongue
is the law of kindness.
Proverbs 31:25-26 NKJV

Then Hannah prayed and said:
"My heart rejoices in the Lord;
in the Lord my horn is lifted high."
1 Samuel 2:1

for Mothers

He Is Strength

The Lord is my strength and my
song; he has become my salvation.
Psalm 118:14

Behold, God is my salvation; I will
trust, and will not be afraid;
for the Lord God is my strength
and my song, and he has
become my salvation.
Isaiah 12:2 RSV

Sing aloud to God our strength;
make a joyful shout to
the God of Jacob.
Psalm 81:1 NKJV

My flesh and my heart fail;
but God is the strength of my
heart and my portion forever.
Psalm 73:26 NKJV

for Mothers

He Gives Strength

You armed me with strength
for battle; you made my
adversaries bow at my feet.
2 Samuel 22:40

It is God that girdeth me
with strength, and maketh
my way perfect.
Psalm 18:32 KJV

He giveth power to the faint;
and to them that have no might
he increaseth strength.
Isaiah 40:29 KJV

God's Little Book of Promises

for Mothers

The Truth about Stress

You will keep in perfect peace him
whose mind is steadfast, because
he trusts in you. Trust in the Lord
forever, for the Lord, the Lord,
is the Rock eternal.
Isaiah 26:3-4

Come to Me, all you who
labor and are heavy laden,
and I will give you rest.
Matthew 11:28 NKJV

May the Lord of peace himself
give you peace at all times
and in every way.
2 Thessalonians 3:16

Moreover, when God gives
any man wealth and possessions,
and enables him to enjoy them,
to accept his lot and be happy in
his work—this is a gift of God.
Ecclesiastes 5:19

for Mothers

Peace in the Midst of Stress

I will listen to what God the Lord
will say; he promises peace to
his people, his saints.
Psalm 85:8

Great peace have they which
love thy law: and nothing
shall offend them.
Psalm 119:165 KJV

Therefore being justified by faith,
we have peace with God through
our Lord Jesus Christ.
Romans 5:1 KJV

And let the peace of God rule
in your hearts, to the which
also ye are called in one body;
and be ye thankful.
Colossians 3:15 KJV

❧

Godly Peace

Lord, you will establish peace
for us, for You have also
done all our works in us.
Isaiah 26:12 NKJV

Consider the blameless,
observe the upright; there is a
future for the man of peace.
Psalm 37:37

"And in this place I will grant
peace," declares the Lord Almighty.
Haggai 2:9

And the peace of God, which
passeth all understanding, shall
keep your hearts and minds
through Christ Jesus.
Philippians 4:7 KJV

The Truth about Success

True humility and respect for the
Lord lead a man to riches,
honor and long life.
Proverbs 22:4 TLB

And, of course, it is very good if a
man has received wealth from the
Lord, and the good health to enjoy
it. To enjoy your work and
to accept your lot in life—
that is indeed a gift from God.
Ecclesiastes 5:19 TLB

You will decide on a matter, and it
will be established for you, and
light will shine on your ways.
Job 22:28 RSV

Riches and honor are with me,
enduring wealth and prosperity.
Proverbs 8:18 RSV

❦

Heavenly Success

He should eat and drink and
enjoy the fruits of his labors,
for these are gifts from God.
Ecclesiastes 3:13 TLB

Wealth and riches are in his house,
and his righteousness
endures forever.
Psalm 112:3

In My Father's house are many
dwelling places; if it were not so,
I would have told you; for I go to
prepare a place for you. If I go
and prepare a place for you,
I will come again and receive
you to Myself, that where I am,
there you may be also.
John 14:2-3 NASB

for Mothers

Earthly Success

The Lord your God will make you
abound in all the work of your
hand, in the fruit of your body,
in the increase of your livestock,
and in the produce of
your land for good.
Deuteronomy 30:9 NKJV

Blessed is every one who fears
the Lord, who walks in His ways.
When you eat the labor of your
hands, you shall be happy,
and it shall be well with you.
Psalm 128:1-2 NKJV

He shall be like a tree planted
by the rivers of water, that brings
forth its fruit in its season, whose
leaf also shall not wither; and
whatever he does shall prosper.
Psalm 1:3 NKJV

The Truth about Suffering

He is despised and rejected
by men, a Man of sorrows
and acquainted with grief.
And we hid, as it were, our faces
from Him; He was despised,
and we did not esteem Him.
Isaiah 53:3 NKJV

He then began to teach them
that the Son of Man must suffer
many things and be rejected by the
elders, chief priests and teachers of
the law, and that he must be killed
and after three days rise again.
Mark 8:31

For as the sufferings of Christ
abound in us, so our consolation
also aboundeth by Christ.
2 Corinthians 1:5 KJV

Surviving Suffering

I delight in weaknesses, in insults,
in hardships, in persecutions,
in difficulties. For when I am
weak, then I am strong.
2 Corinthians 12:10

For I consider that the sufferings
of this present time are not worthy
to be compared with the glory
which shall be revealed in us.
Romans 8:18 NKJV

Thou therefore endure hardness,
as a good soldier of Jesus Christ.
2 Timothy 2:3 KJV

For to you it has been
granted on behalf of Christ,
not only to believe in Him,
but also to suffer for His sake.
Philippians 1:29 NKJV

❦

Triumph over Suffering

A righteous man may have
many troubles, but the Lord
delivers him from them all.
Psalm 34:19

Blessed is the man who endures
temptation; for when he has been
proved, he will receive the crown
of life which the Lord has
promised to those who love Him.
James 1:12 NKJV

Because he himself suffered when
he was tempted, he is able to help
those who are being tempted.
Hebrews 2:18

God's Little Book of Promises

for Mothers

The Truth about Temptation

Put on the whole armor of God,
that you may be able to stand
against the wiles of the devil.
Ephesians 6:11 NKJV

Be self-controlled and alert. Your
enemy the devil prowls around
like a roaring lion looking
for someone to devour.
1 Peter 5:8

The Lord knows how to deliver
the godly out of temptations and to
reserve the unjust under punishment
for the day of judgment.
2 Peter 2:9 NKJV

Watch and pray so that you will
not fall into temptation. The spirit
is willing, but the body is weak.
Mark 14:38

Help for Temptation

No temptation has overtaken you
that is not common to man. God
is faithful, and he will not let you
be tempted beyond your strength,
but with the temptation will also
provide the way of escape, that
you may be able to endure it.
1 Corinthians 10:13 RSV

For since he himself has now been
through suffering and temptation,
he knows what it is like when we
suffer and are tempted, and he is
wonderfully able to help us.
Hebrews 2:18 TLB

You are of God, little children, and
have overcome them, because He
who is in you is greater than
he who is in the world.
1 John 4:4 NKJV

Tempting Others

Therefore let us not judge
one another anymore, but rather
resolve this, not to put a stumbling
block or a cause to fall in
our brother's way.
Romans 14:13 NKJV

Do not cause anyone to stumble,
whether Jews, Greeks or the
church of God.
1 Corinthians 10:32

Let us therefore be diligent
to enter that rest, lest anyone
fall according to the same
example of disobedience.
Hebrews 4:11 NKJV

❧

The Truth about Thankfulness

Let your roots grow down into
him and draw up nourishment
from him. See that you go on
growing in the Lord, and become
strong and vigorous in the truth
you were taught. Let your
lives overflow with joy and
thanksgiving for all he has done.
Colossians 2:7 TLB

And whatever you do or say, let it
be as a representative of the Lord
Jesus, and come with him into the
presence of God the Father to give
him your thanks.
Colossians 3:17 TLB

Give Thanks

Thanks be to God,
who gives us the victory
through our Lord Jesus Christ.
1 Corinthians 15:57 NASB

But thanks be to God, who always
leads us in triumphal procession
in Christ and through us spreads
everywhere the fragrance of
the knowledge of him.
2 Corinthians 2:14

In everything give thanks;
for this is the will of God in
Christ Jesus for you.
1 Thessalonians 5:18 NKJV

Songs of Thanksgiving

Give thanks to the Lord, for he is
good; his love endures forever.
Let them give thanks to the Lord
for his unfailing love and his
wonderful deeds for men.
Psalm 107:1, 21

Then he turned my sorrow into
joy! He took away my clothes of
mourning and clothed me with joy
so that I might sing glad praises to
the Lord. . . . O Lord my God, I
will keep on thanking you forever!
Psalm 30:11-12 TLB

O come, let us sing for joy to the
Lord, let us shout joyfully to the
rock of our salvation. Let us
come before His presence
with thanksgiving.
Psalm 95:1-2 NASB

God's Little Book of Promises

for Mothers

The Truth about Tragedy

Even when walking through the
dark valley of death I will not be
afraid, for you are close beside me,
guarding, guiding all the way.
Psalm 23:4 TLB

Weeping may remain for a night,
but rejoicing comes
in the morning.
Psalm 30:5

When you pass through the
waters, I will be with you;
and through the rivers, they
shall not overflow you. When
you walk through the fire,
you shall not be burned,
nor shall the flame scorch you.
Isaiah 43:2 NKJV

for Mothers

Triumph in Tragedy

He gives power to the tired and
worn out, and strength to the weak.
Isaiah 40:29 TLB

Those who mourn are fortunate!
for they shall be comforted.
Matthew 5:4 TLB

Come to Me, all who are
weary and heavy-laden,
and I will give you rest.
Matthew 11:28 NASB

Let not your heart be troubled;
you believe in God,
believe also in Me.
John 14:1 NKJV

for Mothers

God's Presence in Tragedy

He heals the brokenhearted
and binds up their wounds.
Psalm 147:3 NKJV

Arise, shine; for your light
has come, and the glory of
the Lord has risen upon you.
For behold, darkness will cover
the earth and deep darkness
the peoples; but the Lord
will rise upon you and His
glory will appear upon you.
Isaiah 60:1-2 NASB

For you have been a defense
for the helpless, a defense for the
needy in his distress, a refuge from
the storm, a shade from the heat.
Isaiah 25:4 NASB

The Truth about Wisdom

If you want to know what God
wants you to do, ask him, and he
will gladly tell you, for he is
always ready to give a bountiful
supply of wisdom to all who
ask him; he will not resent it.
James 1:5 TLB

Praise be to the name of God
for ever and ever; wisdom
and power are his. He reveals
deep and hidden things; he
knows what lies in darkness,
and light dwells with him.
Daniel 2:20,22

In whom are hid all the treasures
of wisdom and knowledge.
Colossians 2:3 KJV

The Wisdom of God

I will praise the Lord, who
counsels me; even at night
my heart instructs me.
Psalm 16:7

Yes, if you want better insight and
discernment, and are searching for
them as you would for lost money
or hidden treasure, then wisdom
will be given you, and knowledge
of God himself; you will soon
learn the importance of reverence
for the Lord and of trusting him.
For the Lord grants wisdom! His
every word is a treasure of
knowledge and understanding.
Proverbs 2:3-6 TLB

The Lord by wisdom founded
the earth; by understanding
He established the heavens.
Proverbs 3:19 NKJV

❦

Earthly Wisdom

For the foolishness of God is wiser
than men, and the weakness of
God is stronger than men.
1 Corinthians 1:25 RSV

For since in the wisdom of God the
world through its wisdom did not
come to know God, God was well-
pleased through the foolishness
of the message preached
to save those who believe.
1 Corinthians 1:21 NASB

God has chosen the foolish things
of the world to shame the wise,
and God has chosen the weak
things of the world to shame the
things which are strong.
1 Corinthians 1:27 NASB

Additional copies of this book and
other titles from Honor Books are
available at your local bookstore.

God's Little Book of Promises
God's Little Devotional Bible
God's Little Devotional Book
God's Little Instruction Book

Honor Books
Tulsa, Oklahoma